A very long time ago a group of nomadic hunters made their way from Asia across the frozen Bering Sea and arrived on the American continent. There, they found wide plains, well-stocked waterways, beautiful forests, and plenty of wild animals. They decided to stay. These people had thick black hair and reddish-tan skin. They used to be called Indians; today, they are called Native Americans.

The Native Americans flourished in their new land, and, in time, more than 500 tribes spread across the continent like constellations of stars.

Mason Crest Publishers, Inc.
370 Reed Road
Broomall, Pennsylvania 19008
866-MCP-BOOK (toll free)

Illustrations copyright © 2000 Robert Ingpen
Published in association with Grimm Press Ltd., Taiwan

1 3 5 7 9 8 6 4 2

Library of Congress Cataloging-in-Publication Data:

on file at the Library of Congress.

ISBN 1-59084-154-9
ISBN 1-59084-133-6 (series)

Great Names

CHIEF SEATTLE

Mason Crest Publishers
Philadelphia

Nearly 150 years ago, an old chieftain led his people into the mountains, to look once last time upon the land that had once been theirs. He spoke with sorrow: "Look how blue our harbor is, how it sparkles in the sunlight. Feel the softness of the earth beneath your feet. Smell the piney scent of the morning dew. Look, children, and hold what you see in your heart, for this is our home, where once we were many as the shells upon the sands." The man was Chief Seattle, leader of the Suquamish and Duwamish tribes.

Long ago, their ancestors had settled this land. Every spring, the men fished from their canoes in the salmon-filled waters. They hunted deer and elk in the wooded hills. They salted, smoked, or dried what they caught, to feed

the tribe through
the long, cold winter. They
cut wood from the forests for their
houses and canoes. The women wove clothes
and baskets. But the happiest times were when
they came together to celebrate or to listen to the elders of
the tribe retell the stories of their ancestors.

Chief Seattle's father was a Suquamish chief and his mother was
the daughter of a Duwamish chief. They lived on the northwest coast of
America in an area that is known today as the Puget Sound.

Born around 1786, Chief Seattle learned to hunt and fish from his father, who taught his son to take from the world only what he needed. Seattle learned that it was wrong to use nets that were too fine or to kill too many animals.

When Seattle was six years old, a ship like a white-winged bird sailed into the bay. On board were many strange-looking men. Their skin was white, and their eyes were blue, green, or brown. Some had hair that shone like gold. Others had hair that was as brown as a horse's mane. The men unloaded many strange objects.

The elders of the tribe recognized these strangers as "white men." None of them had ever seen a white man, but they had heard from other tribes about these strangers. They were said to be cunning and fierce. It was even said that they ate people. Many of them carried a long "pipe," which they called a gun. To young Seattle, the gun was a terrifying weapon.

At first, Seattle's people kept their distance. But they soon lost their fear, for the white men were friendly and offered goods in exchange for fish, meat, and other food. The children began to follow them around and talk to them in sign language. They learned that two open hands placed on the head meant they wanted deer meat.

The white men were making a map of the coast. When it was finished, they would be able to navigate the bay safely. Seattle wondered how many more white men would come and what they would bring when they returned.

In 1792, Captain George Vancouver, of the *H. M. S. Discovery*, led a voyage to survey and chart the Pacific Coast of North America.

The white men soon sailed away, and the tribe returned to its life of hunting and fishing. The days passed, and Seattle grew bigger and stronger. No one could shoot an arrow straighter or gallop faster than he could. In time, he became the chief of his tribe and the leader of five other tribes.

During these years, more white settlers and traders came by wagon, horse, and boat. They built their houses and fenced in the land for their livestock. The natives couldn't understand why they called the land their "property." But Chief Seattle was very friendly with the white settlers because he remembered the kind white faces of the men from his childhood.

The white men traded with Chief Seattle's people, buying fish and wood in exchange for metal tools. When the white men decided to establish a settlement, Chief Seattle suggested they build a trading post with a postal service and a place for travelers and traders to stay on the east side of the Puget Sound. In appreciation for Chief Seattle's support, the settlement was named "Seattle." The chief never imagined how quickly the white people's villlage would grow or how it would engulf his people.

The white men established their first settlement near the Puget Sound in 1851, and in 1852, they renamed it Seattle in recognition of the chief's friendship. Today, the old trading post lies in the heart of the city of Seattle.

As the white men pushed into native lands, disagreements increased. White hunters slaughtered the game that had once been plentiful, making it hard for native hunters to feed their families. White men cut down the forests to make way for the railroad. Worst of all, they had no respect for the land, which had nourished generations of native people. They even destroyed the graves of the natives' ancestors.

Among Chief Seattle's neighbors, hunger and anger flared into hatred. The warriors wanted to force the white men to leave, but they met with fierce resistance. The white settlers fought back, and the once peaceful land ran with blood.

It was not long before these problems arrived at Chief Seattle's door as well. One day, white officials came and politely but firmly informed him that the United States government planned to buy the lands his people had lived on for thousands of years. In return, it would reserve other land for the tribe.

As the message left the mouth of the translator, Chief Seattle saw the angry eyes of his young people. But as an old man, he listened with sorrow, not anger. He knew that anger and hatred would only bring pain to his people. More important, he knew that the white soldiers greatly outnumbered his warriors. There was no hope of defeating them. He thought, "Like a wounded doe, we can do nothing but listen to the approaching steps of the hunter."

When the white officials pressed Chief Seattle for an answer, he slowly rose to his feet and, pointing at the sky, he gave his reply. (The following words are a free adaptation of Chief Seattle's original speech):

The sky has wept compassionate tears
on us for centuries;
it looks eternal, but it changes.
My words are like stars that never set.
For us, the sky and earth are the origins of life.
A flower or a leaf holds our memories;
An insect or horse contains
The tales of our past.

Have you heard the sounds of a brook?

My people believe the streams are sacred.

Clear rivers reflected the faces of our ancestors;

The murmurs of the stream are the patient reminders of them.

When we are thirsty, it refreshes us.

When we are hungry, it provides us with food.

It even embraces our canoes with its tender arms.

It is not merely a river, but our endearing brother.

Have you ever smelled the sweet breeze

or the damp, fresh fragrance

of the earth in the afternoon?

My people believe the air is sacred.

It endows us with breath and fragrance.

It sends trees, animals, insects, and

the beautiful gift of breath and fragrance.

From birth until death, it lives with us.

What is more valuable than this?

Have you touched the trunk of a tree or a blade of grass?

Do you feel the sap in them,

just like the blood within us?

Humans, animals, plants, rivers, and mountains

all belong to earth,

and earth belongs to us as well.

Earth is our mother.

Flowers are our sisters.

Animals are our brothers.

We are a big family.

We share sunshine, raindrops, and the earth.

The earth breeds us.

And we add energies to the earth.

Then, white people appeared.

Buffalo died under white people's guns,

buffalo bodies slaughtered in the sunlight.

Trees fell under white men's axes;

forests turned into bare desert.

Our brothers and sisters are gone.

Our mother carries ugly injuries.

We are the orphans left behind by the earth.

We can never ride our horses roaming on the plain.

And we can never hear the songs of the wind again.

When you asked me to sell the land to the white people,

My people could not understand it.

How can you buy the sky and the earth?

They do not belong to anyone.

My people do not believe

that white people can take over the sky

and rule the earth.

Think about this:

If the buffalos are all dead,

if the horses are all gone,

can you buy them back?

White people treat the earth and sky as merchandise.

My people are heartbroken.

Perhaps for white people the earth is not their friend, but their enemy.

They destroy the earth with guns and weapons.

They chop down the trees and kill the animals.

They move on without looking back

and set out to search for a new land.

They know nothing about true treasure.

If we sell the land to you,

remember the earth is sacred.

Remember the animals are our brothers.

And the flowers and the trees are our sisters.

Love the earth like you guard your mother,

and set this as a model for your children.

Everything is connected.

If we hurt the earth,

we also devastate our own roots in this world.

When Chief Seattle was finished, he searched the faces of the white officials. Had they understood? Did his words mean anything to them?

The government moved quickly to carry out its plan, moving Chief Seattle's people off their land and onto a reservation. He was the first chief to sign the treaty—many others refused. One solemn day, he led his tribe way from their home to their new life on the reservation, saying, "Look for one last time upon your mother, your brothers, your sisters. Young warriors from many tribes have sworn to join together and fight, but that path will bring nothing but sorrow. We must lay down our knives. The white men must lay down their guns. All of us must learn to live in harmony with the earth and each other."

Epilogue:

Chief Seattle lived the rest of his life on the reservation. When the tribes of the Washington Territories banded together to fight the United States government, neither he nor his people joined them. He died in 1866.

Dr. Henry Smith had accompanied the governor on his visit to the tribes of the Puget Sound, and, on October 29, 1887, his record of Chief Seattle's speech appeared in the *Seattle Sunday Star*. This was the earliest and most accurate version of the chief's speech. In later years, many other adaptations were written and published.

Today, the beautiful city of Seattle is one of great diversity. And today's Native Americans are rebuilding their culture, preserving their traditions, and writing their own histories.

Chief Seattle is still with us. Through his speech, he lives on as a guide to living in harmony with the earth. As he himself said, "My words are like the stars. They do not set."

BIOGRAPHIES

Author Anna Carew-Miller is a freelance writer and former teacher, who lives in rural northwestern Connecticut with her husband and daughter. Although she has a Ph.D. in American Literature and has done extensive research and writing on literary topics, more recently, Anna has written books for younger readers.

Illustrator Robert Ingpen was born in 1936 in Geelong, Australia. Ingpen's earliest work was the sketch of a shell he did when he was young. His first job, at the age of 22, was to draw illustrations and design publicity pamphlets for CSIRO, a scientific research institution. All of his illustrations were related to various scientific research reports. The work honed his perception and established his realistic style of painting. Interestingly, Ingpen's illustrations sometimes inspired scientists to explore and study the subject at hand from new perspectives. This is where the charm of Ingpen lies.